RUSTIC WEDDING CHIC

RUSTIC WEDDING CHIC

MAGGIE LORD

Editor of RusticWeddingChic.com

GIBBS SMITH
TO ENRICH AND INSPIRE HUMANKIND

First Edition
16 15 14 13 12   5 4 3 2 1

Text © 2012 Maggie Lord
Photographs © 2012 as noted on page 160

Published by
Gibbs Smith
P.O. Box 667
Layton, Utah 84041

1.800.835.4993 orders
www.gibbs-smith.com

Designed by Tracy Sunrize Johnson
Printed and bound in Hong Kong
Gibbs Smith books are printed on paper produced from sustainable PEFC-certified forest/controlled wood source. Learn more at www.pefc.org.

Library of Congress Cataloging-in-Publication Data

Lord, Maggie.
  Rustic wedding chic / Maggie Lord. — 1st ed.
    p. cm.
  ISBN 978-1-4236-3068-5
1. Weddings—Planning. I. Title.
  HQ745.L67 2012
  395.2'2—dc23
                        2012009987

Half title page: A rustic chic bride relaxes in a vintage-style green pickup truck.

Title page: The classic white wedding cake becomes a rustic cake with the addition of a tree slice cake stand and is topped off with fresh flowers.

To my niece, Aidan Elsie Panian,
who reminds me that true beauty comes
from being exactly who you are.

ACKNOWLEDGMENTS

Thank you to the Rustic Wedding Chic readers, contributors and supporters; without you, none of this would be possible.

Thank you to the contributing photographers, flower designers, event planners, artists and others who provided the beautiful inspiration. Especially, Ash and James Photography, Brklyn View Photography, Carrie Wildes, Charlie Panian, ee Photography, Hinkley Photo, Kate Holstein Photography, Krista Lee Photography, Kristyn Hogan, Mirelle Carmichael Photography, Orchard Cove Photography, Our Labor of Love Photography, Revival Photography, Sparkle Photography, Tahni Candelaria-Holm, Tom Moore Photo, Vanessa Joy. And a special thank-you to Virginia and Chelsea with Bluebird Productions and Catherine from Farm Couture Living for their wonderful insights and informative additions to the book.

Thank you to Meghan Schaetzle and Marisa Beltramini for their dedication and hard work.

Thank you to Mary Louise Dudley who brought a world of knowledge and a sense of direction to the project.

My sincerest thanks to the entire team at Gibbs Smith for their professional support and dedication. Especially my editors, Hollie Keith and Madge Baird, for fostering this project through the many stages.

Thank you to my family who has supported all of my entrepreneurial endeavors dating back to "Maggie's Shell Shop."

Thank you, Mickey Kelly Murray, who a long time ago introduced me to what rustic and chic really means.

I'd like to also thank Susan Kelly Panian for providing a fundamental base of love, guidance and confidence and whose optimism is unwavering, and Ed Panian for always contributing a creative spirit.

Edward and Charlie Panian, thank you for your technical help, artistic instruction, inspiration and for believing in the blog from the earliest of days. Thank you to my nephew, Eddie, whose imagination and spirit reminds me to dream big; Jen Pokorney who is always there with a hot meal and sound advice; and to my grandmother, Mariann Kelly, for her wisdom, style and unconditional love.

To my husband, Jon, who supported me through the days of planning our own rustic wedding and every day since.

And lastly, to my son, Jack, who played at my feet while this book was written and who brings me endless joy.

Below: A country chic bride and groom take a moment's rest at their outdoor wedding.

Facing, left: A few perfectly placed bright flowers are mixed with red berries in this rustic wedding bouquet.

Facing, center: A bride's rustic bouquet looks perfectly in place upon a painted wood chair.

Facing, right: Wooden directional signs add both country charm and are also helpful for your guests, especially when your wedding is on a larger piece of property such as a farm.

CONTENTS

INTRODUCTION

A rustic wedding is a state of mind, an overall aesthetic and feeling woven through the many beautiful moments of a wedding. The word *rustic* implies a whole world of possibilities. Just as endless as a bride's expectations, so too are the various forms a rustic wedding can take. Now more than ever, couples are yearning to place their own original stamp on their weddings in hopes of creating a more unique and personalized experience. It is this desire for a more original ceremony that often leads couples to the wonderful and expansive world of rustic weddings.

Perhaps what comes to mind when you think of rustic weddings are locations like barns, mountaintops, fields and orchards, or details like wood beams, tiny lights, magical table décor and thoughtful favors. While all of these examples are true, the real beauty of a rustic wedding is its versatility. Rustic weddings come in all shapes, sizes and price ranges. The weddings you will see in this book are as unique as the couples who planned them. I have seen couples make almost any setting feel rustic, from traditional country venues such as farms, barns, lodges and vineyards to family backyards, extravagant resorts and even urban hotels.

As a couple, you should first strive to define the essence of your style. Once you have an idea of what you want, you can easily take the rustic-style elements that fit your taste and adapt them to your own venue and budget with a fresh and personalized twist. As you will experience throughout the book, rustic weddings can be many

Facing: A long pathway of trees acts as a wonderful symbol of the journey of marriage this new bride and groom are embarking on.

Below: Here is a white lace wedding gown in the still moments before the bride starts her getting-ready process.

things because their beauty is never limited. The fantasy of your dream rustic wedding is yours to have.

You may now be saying to yourself that all of this is easier said than done. The story of your wedding day is yet to be written and there are endless possibilities, with inevitably some twists and turns along the way. Almost every couple will admit that the time leading up to their big day includes some of the most stressful moments of their lives, but planning a wedding should be fun. Allow yourself to get excited about the fact that your wedding is one of the few days in your life when you are able to curate the entire experience, from start to finish. Relaxing and enjoying the overall process is crucial to making the day a success. And there's no reason to be afraid of imperfections. In fact, sometimes it's those obstacles that make for the most memorable moments. Every wedding, no matter how flawless the planning, has its fair share of wrinkles and quirks. Embrace each moment, perfect or not, as one small piece of fabric that, when sewn together, creates a wonderful patchwork quilt of memories you will cherish for a lifetime.

A wedding gives you the opportunity to express your love and to realize your creative ideas, so your big day makes a true and unique statement about your bond. A marriage is the union of two individuals who wish to spend their lives together. A wedding, on the other hand, is the joyous celebration of this union and should reflect both of you as individuals and as the couple you form. Remember that you are inviting your wedding guests to share in the celebration of your love and it is so much more than the dress, cake or flowers. Even though each of these details is important, it's key not to lose sight of the fact that on your wedding day you should be surrounded by the people you love and the things that make you the happiest. By being true to yourself and letting your imagination flow, you can bring this special day to life.

I created the Rustic Wedding Chic blog when I was in the process of planning my own wedding. My husband and I knew that we wanted our wedding to be personal, unique and, above all, our own. At the same time, we wanted to provide a wonderful and rich experience for our family and friends who would all be traveling to the tiny Midwest town where

Facing, upper: A rustic bride and groom create juxtaposition between the wedding elegance and the rustic natural wood.

Facing, lower: The gold tones in this couple's wedding dresses complement each other.

my family has had a summer home for the past sixty years. By first starting with the big picture, planning a lakeside wedding, I was then able to focus on the smaller details such as a canoe filled with drinks, resting on the shore of the lake, where we would arrive by boat after our church ceremony. Visions like these formed an entire rustic wedding slideshow in my mind. All I needed to find were some real-life examples that I could use to make my dream a reality.

When I was planning my wedding, I was in need of not only inspiration but also the practical advice that would help me create my big day. I spent a lot of time reading many different wedding blogs, but I was always disappointed by the lack of information about rustic weddings. So I set out to create a blog that would speak to these specific types of brides. The original vision for my blog still holds true today: to make Rustic Wedding Chic a daily muse for brides, couples and wedding enthusiasts, offering an online venue for idea gathering and inspiration.

I am so honored to now add the Rustic Wedding Chic book to the collection of resources I can provide for couples as they start to plan their own rustic weddings. The idea for a Rustic Wedding Chic book grew out of the popularity of the blog and from interested readers who asked for a more comprehensive collection of wedding features. Serving as an extension of the blog, this *Rustic Wedding Chic* book offers you some of our finest rustic weddings, "inspiration shoots," "get the look" ideas, advice and resources. I hope you find this book as inspiring as it was for me to put together. Remember to slow down and take the time to find joy in planning your own rustic wedding, a celebration that we here at Rustic Wedding Chic hope will serve as the first of many happy toasts to come.

Above, left: This bride created a memory tree by adding pictures from both families along with their families' wedding pictures.

Above, right: This bride sports a bright red sweater that adds a pop of color against the fall foliage.

REAL WEDDINGS

Let's face it. At one time or another, we have all attended a wedding and been charmed by a special detail, made a mental note and tucked it away for our own wedding day. Whether it was a unique wedding cake, a breathtaking dress or a clever design element that made everyone " " and "ahh," there is something both fun and inspiring about seeing how other couples put the pieces together to build their perfect day. With the planning process as overwhelming as it is, you're not only expected but also strongly encouraged to borrow ideas from other couples. In fact, some of the best ideas for your wedding will come from other weddings. Getting the chance to see how real brides have brought their rustic wedding to life will give you even more enthusiasm for planning your own wedding and serve as a jumping-off point for further inspiration.

This section is a wonderful invitation for an insider's look at some of the most beautiful rustic weddings across the country, complete with all those small details that personalize the experience and make the day a lasting memory from start to finish. By exploring weddings featuring real couples, in real venues with real emotion, you get a true sense for the wedding. Such an intimate look at real weddings will inspire you to start taking the rustic-style elements that you like the best and applying them to your own special day. We hope this section leaves you not only inspired but also convinced that, with a little planning, any great idea is doable. Enjoy the chance to get a front-row seat to these real rustic weddings and start taking notes!

A bride carries a sunflower wedding bouquet with her groom on a rustic dirt road.

Northwoods Camp

Set on the shores of a northern Wisconsin lake, this affair has all the fixings for a perfect rustic wedding! Selecting a location that holds a special place for the groom's family, this couple chose to have a Hindu ceremony lakeside followed by a classic camp-style lodge reception. With the autumn season as their backdrop, the couple filled their wedding day with camp style and DIY details.

This lodge-style reception with rock fireplace not only looks rustic but also looks sweet with guests holding handmade signs.

Above: This outdoor wedding ceremony in northern Wisconsin has a tranquil lakeside setting.

Right: A wedding held at a summer camp adds for amusing details such as a "Swim At Your Own Risk" sign.

Right: Camps can be the perfect place for a rustic wedding. Camp Nawakwa in northern Wisconsin is a great example of a nontraditional wedding venue.

Below, left: Held at a local summer camp in northern Wisconsin, this wedding has a classic relaxed rustic style complete with burlap table runners.

Below, right: Invite your guests to have a good time with upbeat sayings displayed on wood signs.

Facing, upper: The bride and groom's names are proudly displayed on a burlap banner in addition to a mantel filled with special memories.

Facing, lower: A bride and groom show off their respective wedding day shoes.

Above: The color red decorates a bride's nails, a hair accessory and a bouquet mixed with brightly colored flowers.

Facing: This strapless wedding gown with a sweetheart neckline looks flawless in the woods of northern Wisconsin.

Above, left: Coffee in a classic souvenir mug acts as the perfect camp wedding favor.

Above, right: Nontraditional bands such as a bluegrass band, a folk band or a country band can really help bring a rustic wedding to life with music.

Facing: Orange and white pumpkins complete a minimalist look as they fit right in with this fall centerpiece idea.

Facing: This bride and groom take a moment to be surrounded by the natural beauty of the woods at their camp-style wedding.

Above: A summer camp's dining hall is transformed into a rustic wedding venue.

SOURCES

Photography: Ash and James Photography
Venue: YMCA Camp Nawakwa
Catering: Bad Bones BBQ, Inc.
Florist: Crystal Marie's Floral

Enchanted Garden

Nestled in the North Carolina mountains
on the famous Biltmore Estate, this romantic
wedding creates the feeling of being in an
enchanted garden. With dramatic candlelight, an
abundance of flowers and dazzling table décor,
the atmosphere is like a dreamland.

Wood arbor structures are a great way to create a
focal point at your wedding ceremony.

Facing, upper: A lace ribbon enhances the bride's bouquet and adds a vintage feel. Wrap your wedding bouquet with a piece of lace from your mother or grandmother's wedding gown and let it be your "something borrowed."

Facing, lower: Displaying flowers in a variety of vases creates a less stylized look and helps to achieve a more natural look. This bride chose to line the wedding aisle with not only different styles of vases but also various types of flowers and at varying heights.

Right: This timeless-looking bride has a wedding day portrait in a classic country setting.

Above, left: Blush-tone flowers are mixed with blue and green hues to create a lovely balance and are displayed beautifully in a rustic birch vase.

Above, right: This elaborate centerpiece creates height and depth to the long wedding table with candles and flowers at different heights.

Facing, left: Adding drapes to a rustic setting can soften the rustic qualities and add airiness to help achieve a more elegant look and feel.

Facing, right: Pillar candles and tiny white lights produce soft light that helps to accomplish an intimate reception space.

Above: Tiny white lights frame a fairy-tale-like garden-style wedding reception.

Facing: A bride is walked down the aisle of her indoor rustic wedding ceremony complete with candles and white lights.

SOURCES

Photography: Krista Lee
Venue: Biltmore Estate
Florist: The Bloom Room

Hometown Farm Style

A New Hampshire farm that just happened to be the childhood home of the bride served as the venue for this farm-style wedding. The setting featured an outdoor ceremony and a classic tented reception. Subtle rustic touches such as wooden directional signs and place cards displayed on a fence bring the farm style to life.

A relaxed bride and groom walk through the fields after their outdoor wedding ceremony.

Left: A Vermont farm wedding ceremony takes place on the lawn outside a barn.

Below: Perfectly in balance with the natural surroundings, Emily and Chris inform their guests of the way to their wedding.

Facing, upper: A rustic chic wedding party is complete with bridesmaids in a variety of dress styles and the groom and groomsmen in suspenders.

Facing, lower: Elegant wedding escort cards are hung from a horse-farm-style fence with mini clothespins. This is a wonderful example of how to incorporate natural surroundings into your wedding day design.

Above: Simple and classic wedding table numbers are accompanied by a stunning leaf-wrapped centerpiece.

Right: Green, pink and a pop of purple make for a striking country wedding bouquet.

Facing, upper: This outdoor farm wedding ceremony keeps decorations to a minimum, allowing the natural beauty to be the main backdrop.

Facing, lower left: Get creative with your wedding menu and place settings. Adding small touches such as a piece of twine will help continue and carry out your rustic theme.

Facing, lower right: By including dark wood Chiavari chairs and large natural-looking decorations, this tented reception stays true to the farm-style wedding theme.

Above, left: Staying true to a horse farm theme, this couple found a clever way to display and keep the wind from getting the best of their wedding programs.

Above, right: A wooden ceremony sign points guests in the right direction.

Facing: This couple poses with the bride's horse at their farm-style wedding.

SOURCES

Photography: Orchard Cove Photography
Venue: Bride's childhood home
Catering: Lake Sunapee Country Club
Florist: Art of Nature
Band: The Pulse of Boston
Dress: Melissa Sweet
Bridesmaid Dress: J.Crew
Hair & Makeup: Hair Daze
Invitations: Griffin-Vites
Calligraphy: Dancing Pen Calligraphy
Rental: Lake Region Tent

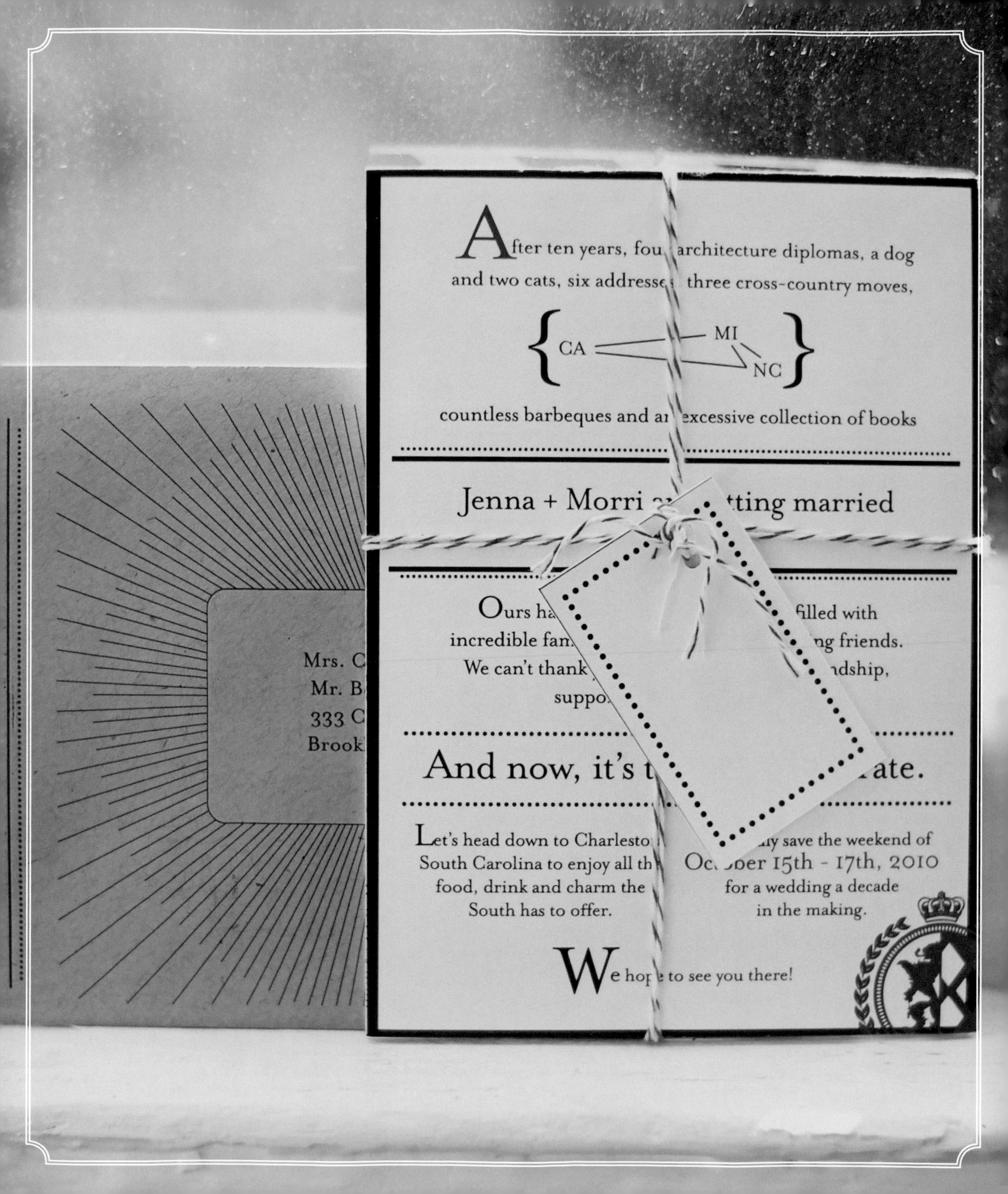

After ten years, four architecture diplomas, a dog
and two cats, six addresses, three cross-country moves,

{ CA — MI
NC }

countless barbeques and an excessive collection of books

Jenna + Morris are getting married

Ours has been a life filled with
incredible family and amazing friends.
We can't thank you enough for your friendship,
support,

And now, it's time to celebrate.

Let's head down to Charleston, please save the weekend of
South Carolina to enjoy all the October 15th - 17th, 2010
food, drink and charm the for a wedding a decade
South has to offer. in the making.

We hope to see you there!

Mrs. C
Mr. B
333 C
Brook

Modern Vintage

Classic vintage styling meets modern freshness at this South Carolina wedding. A navy-and-white color scheme is paired with details such as a book motif that brings this southern wedding to life.

A truly individual and unique wedding invitation tied with string.

Facing, upper: A simple yet elegant garden-style wedding ceremony is held at a wedding venue in Charleston, South Carolina.

Facing, lower: A mostly classic white bridal bouquet and an upbeat and bright bridesmaid's bouquet are placed in mason jars of water.

Above: A navy-and-white theme is carried throughout the wedding stationery for this modern vintage-style wedding.

Above: A stylized welcome poster is paired with a vintage-style book to help greet guests.

Right: Fruit, flowers and books are all mixed together to create an eclectic centerpiece.

Above: This bride carried out her navy-and-white theme by adding a ribbon to her bouquet.

Facing: Bride and groom share a happy moment along a tree-lined path.

Above, left: Incorporating a motif such as the one this couple did adds personality to otherwise plain table number cards.

Above, right: Wedding guests toast one another at understated but chic long tables.

Facing: A modern-style strapless wedding gown looks both sophisticated and stylish.

SOURCES

Photography: Our Labor of Love
Venue: The Governor Thomas
Bennett House
Wedding Designers: Jenna Gibson,
Morri Freeman and Whitney Gibson
of Blue Lemon Provisions
Wedding Planner: Whitney Gibson
of Blue Lemon Provisions
Day of Coordination: Emmy Brooks
and Ashley Ruthsatz
Stationery Design: Jenna Gibson
and Morri Freeman of Blue Lemon
Provisions
Stationery Letterpress: Whitney
Gibson of Blue Lemon Provisions
Florist: Whitney Randall Branch
Design Studio
Wedding Dress: Vera Wang
Hair: Stella Nova
Makeup: Pamela Lesch
Catering: Good Food Catering

Vineyard Beauty

When your wedding is held in a place where
there is nothing but beauty for as far as the eye
can see, you know the wedding is going to be
stunning. Just a short distance away from New
York City, this vineyard location in the Hamptons
acted as a mini-destination wedding. With
the radiant sun shining on acres of vineyards,
this wedding is like being swept away to Tuscany.

With the vineyard in the background, this outdoor
wedding reception is stunning.

Above, left: The bride and her bridesmaid share a laugh at this outdoor wedding.

Above, right: Offer parasols to your guests to provide shade on a hot day.

Facing: Light suits for the men and white dresses for the ladies are both great picks for a wedding in the summer months.

Left: A New York vineyard is the setting for this outdoor sit-down dinner.

Above, left: Make sure your guests stay warm by providing wraps for them. At my own lakeside wedding, I kept my guests warm by displaying a large basket of pashminas with a sign that read: "stay cozy."

Above, right: An elegant wedding table is set with etched drinking glasses and wooden chargers.

Facing: Bride and groom pose as the sun beings to set after their wedding ceremony.

Above: A punch of color is added by pink and green flowers with a few yellow flowers mixed in.

SOURCES

Photography: Our Labor of Love
Venue: Wolffer Estate Vineyard
Dress: Monique Lhuillier
Bridesmaid Dress: Thread
Stationery: The Village Invites
Florist: Claire Bean
Day of Coordination: Claire Bean
Rental: Classic Party Rentals
Catering: Fresh Flavors

Apple Orchard

Soft light, a poetic location and a graceful bride
are the foundation of this magical wedding.
The different-colored bridesmaids' dresses
create a kaleidoscope of colors and, when teamed
with the clean and crisp look of baby's breath,
create a stunning effect.

Adding a photo prop such as a bike can bring some
vintage touches to otherwise very traditional-style
wedding pictures.

Facing, upper: If you desire a less formal and standard type of wedding photo, find a unique location such as an apple orchard for picture taking.

Facing, lower: A very simple wedding bouquet showcases mainly white flowers with just a few added green ones.

Left: A dreamy-looking bride embraces with her new husband.

Facing: A bride kicks back in her boots for a few moments of tranquility.

Above: Low-hanging mist from the hills makes for a dramatic wedding portrait.

Facing, upper left: Having brides-maids in a variety of dress colors is a wonderful way to add personality to a wedding's color theme. When working this idea into your wedding, remember to use a flower such as baby's breath and to keep the bridesmaids' flowers simple so that the bouquet does not clash with one of the colors.

Facing, upper right: A white wedding cake with fresh flowers and a bird cake topper are the perfect pick for a relaxed rustic wedding.

Facing, lower left: Mason jars have countless uses at a wedding since they can be used as candleholders, drinking glasses or vases.

Facing, lower right: Repurpose an old suitcase into a collection spot for your wedding cards.

Above: A "just married" burlap sign hangs from the couple's sweet-heart table at their rustic wedding reception.

SOURCES

Photography: Revival Photography
Venue: Doc & Merle Watson Theatre
Catering: Wilkes Community College Catering
Florist: Cline's Florist
Decorative Banners & Boutonnieres: aPearantly Sew

Farm Fresh

A quintessential barn acts as the backdrop
for this flawless outdoor farm wedding.
From the bride's simple vintage-inspired style
to the understated table décor, this wedding
defines the new fresh farm style.

A classic red-and-white barn acts as the perfect
backdrop for this Virginia wedding.

Facing, upper: These nontraditional boutonnieres add a pop of color to the groom and groomsmen's suits.

Facing, lower: An eclectic band is the perfect complement to a farm-style outdoor wedding ceremony.

Above: Large flower illustrations in muted colors adorn a rustic wedding invitation.

Above: A country bridal gown is surrounded by the bridesmaids' dresses pre-ceremony.

Facing: A country farm bride and groom take in the scenery.

Above: A mix of large and small blooms adds depth to this farm bride's bouquet.

Facing, upper: The bride and groom have a tender moment in a classic farm setting.

Facing, lower: Stylish shoes adorn the feet of this bride and groom on their perfect day.

Upper: This wooden wedding sign looks perfectly in place among the natural wood setting.

Lower: A simple piece of wood is a perfect place to display a table number, and the centerpiece is made up of an assortment of tea lights.

A shawl-wrapped bride and groom leave their wedding with a dramatic sparkler send-off.

Above, left: A light pink bridesmaid dress is paired with a matching pink bouquet and minimal yet beautiful jewelry.

Above, right: Bring ceremony flowers closer to eye level by hanging them from plant stands in small jars.

Facing: A bride and groom share their first dance under a rustic twig-and-branch arrangement embellished with lights.

SOURCES

Photography: Joyeuse Photography
Venue: Inn at Westwood Farm
Dress: BHLDN
Catering: Harvest Moon Catering
Florist: Sugar Magnolias

Country Road

The timeless beauty of the American countryside
is the perfect setting for this sophisticated yet
simple wedding. Majestic trees and a sweeping lawn
surround the charming tented-style reception with
refined details that complement the natural setting.

A bride and groom take a moment on a tree-lined
country road.

Facing: Neutral-colored bridesmaid dresses stand out against the rich natural colors of the country setting.

Above, left: Fun country décor is added to the blank canvas of the tent. Banner flags, large three-dimensional table numbers and even Scrabble letter place cards all add personal touches.

Above, right: Adding distinctive pieces such as typewriters or stick pencils make for fun props at stations like the guestbook signing table.

Above: Items such as this old-fashioned wagon can
be repurposed into handy drink stations.

Facing: A sprawling country location is the backdrop for this tented wedding reception.

Facing: Pre-ceremony, the bride's wedding gown is ready and waiting.

Above: The bride's bouquet is wrapped with a lace handkerchief.

SOURCES

Photography: ee Photography
Venue: Crossed Keys Inn
Dress: Wtoo by Watters
Invitations: Wedding Chicks and Paper Source

Wrapped in Love

A Vermont lakeside resort was the scene of this
picturesque New England mountain wedding.
Due to unpredictable fall temperatures,
a basket appropriately displayed a sign that read:
"Happiness Is a Warm Blanket." The blankets
were used by the guests, wedding party
and even the bride to keep warm.

Husband and wife embrace in front of the birch
ceremony centerpiece.

Above, left: Bridesmaids stand ready with large baskets of flowers.

Above, right: When planning an outdoor wedding, always take into account the comfort of your guests. This bride offered guests warm blankets because of the chilly fall temperature.

Facing, upper: On the shores of the lake, the bride and groom share a kiss.

Facing, lower: A whimsical lake illustration invites guests to this wedding weekend.

Right: A majestic Vermont lake acts as the backdrop for this fall outdoor wedding.

Facing, upper left: Cloth slippers offer guests a way to dance the night away in style. These slippers are fitting for the fall season as apposed to the popular flip-flop options usually seen at summer weddings.

Facing, upper right: Perched on a hill overlooking a lake, this outdoor rustic ceremony is enhanced by rich fall colors.

Facing, lower left: A galvanized bucket is the perfect complement to fall wedding flowers.

Facing, lower right: Creative table names are positioned with large floral centerpieces.

Below: Wrapped in a bright white ribbon, this fall wedding bouquet may only have a few small colored flowers, but they make an impressive impact.

Right: Wrapped in blankets for warmth, the wedding party poses on the pier of a lake.

Facing, upper: By thinking outside the box about traditional wedding flowers, you might be surprised at what sort of bouquet can be put together. These berry bouquets are a perfect example of how amazing and unconventional a bouquet can look.

Facing, lower: With a simple burlap background, these clothespin clips offer a great place card display.

Above: A detailed invitation outlines the weekend's events that include a dockside welcome dinner, wedding and brunch.

SOURCES

Photography: Orchard Cove Photography
Venue: Basin Harbor Club
Florist: Blomma Flicka Florist
Band: Sultans of Swing
Dress: Sassi Holford
Bridesmaids' Dresses: J.Crew
Hair: Erin McKenna
Makeup: Heather Garrow of Makeup Artist Guild
Invitations: Shindig Invites
Birch Structure: Vermont Rustic Cedar
Rental: Vermont Tent Company
Photo Booth: Vermont Photo Booth Company

INSPIRATIONS

Being able to start from scratch is one of the wonderful things about a wedding, but it can also be one of the most daunting. You begin with a blank canvas and must then add your own colors, visions and ideas, one at a time. For brides who might not know where to begin, one great resource is an inspiration shoot. An inspiration shoot is a stylized, fictional wedding with a specific theme running through it, much like a real wedding. Many wedding photographers put together inspiration shoots as a way to help brides explore themes and focus on the details of their weddings. This section is dedicated to beautiful inspirations from some of our favorite photographers. We've covered everything from a burlap-and-white theme to a brightly colored outdoor setting to give you some real creative food for thought!

A casual-looking groom with a fedora takes the hand of his bride.

White & Burlap

The combination of white flowers, dramatic
candlelight and rugged burlap create a simple
yet elegant statement. Elements such as table
runners, chair sashes and invitations,
all made from the natural fabric, complete the
rustic chic look.

A single piece of burlap is wrapped around the
bride's chair.

Facing: An antique white décor element brings to life a vintage chic quality.

Above: A burlap-wrapped invitation has a rugged rustic touch but is elegant enough for a wedding.

Above: Loose crystals and metallic stones are scattered up and down a long farm-style table. Small white bags add a refined look and help to balance the rugged look of the burlap table runner.

Facing, left: This classic-style chandelier looks right at home in this rustic setting.

Facing, right: A white color theme can be carried past the table décor and onto the surrounding fixtures.

Above, left: These baby's breath arrangements in garden-style pots offer a less formal yet stylish feel to the table décor.

Above, right: A burlap-and-white decorated table gets a little extra sparkle with the added crystal detailing.

Facing: The white wedding cake looks stylish and elegant with minimal embellishments.

SOURCES

Photography: Kristyn Hogan
Venue: Cedarwood
Styling & Floral Design: Cedarwood
Stationery: Designs In Paper
Cake: Patty Cakes

Fish Camp

This 1940s-style rehearsal dinner inspiration shoot is reminiscent of the old-fashioned fish camps where families would gather in the summer to enjoy nature's bounty. Allowing the natural beauty to act as the main décor centerpiece, this understated affair conveys a timeless quality.

Bottles filled with flowers seem to float above the table, as they are tied with twine from the towering tree above.

Left: This inspiration shoot shows just how intimate a rehearsal dinner can be. After all, it's really about getting a group of friends and family together to celebrate the time before the wedding.

Above: This menu sign is a great DIY project. Find a small, round piece of wood, sand it down a bit and then paint the front with chalkboard paint.

Facing, upper: This beautiful mint green rehearsal dinner invitation is both rustic and elegant.

Facing, lower left: Adding a little plant or flower to each place setting can really enhance a table and provides a major impact for relatively low cost.

Facing, lower right: A repurposed anchor welcomes guests at this lakeside rehearsal dinner.

Above: Even in the outdoors, items such as china cabinets can look perfectly in place when filled with the right wedding trappings.

Right: Items such as classic-style fish creels and poles are perfect rustic wedding props and might be as easy to find as looking in your own attic.

SOURCES

Photography: ee Photography / *Venue:* Five Chimney Inn
Event Design: Shelbi Rampy of Events By Shelbi Rene
Paper Products: Three by the Quill Pen
Dessert Design: Kendra Heard of Skunk and Bee

Happy Trails

The beauty of the trails meets the romance of the west in this equestrian-style inspiration. This chic boho bride and groom add plenty of style drama with her oversized turquoise necklace and his fedora.

Posing with a horse may not be the most conventional type of wedding picture, but the end result is a beautiful unique memory.

Left: This inspiration shoot confirms how a casually dressed groom can look wedding ready when standing next to a beautiful bride.

Facing, upper: Small individual cakes are a creative way to serve your guests dessert.

Facing, lower: A large piece of jewelry such as this stunning turquoise necklace provides lots of drama and makes quite a statement.

Facing: Even in a barn, chandeliers add elegance and romance.

Above: If you can select a setting such as a meadow for your pictures, you might be lucky enough to end up with amazing knee-high flowers as shown in this inspiration shoot.

SOURCES

Photography: ee Photography
Cakes: The Cupcake Lounge
Stylist: Crystal Duran

Bright, Bold & Beautiful

A wedding inspiration filled with bright, bold and beautiful colors shows off the vibrant side of a rustic wedding. This inspiration features both an indoor and outdoor venue and color for days. A farm table decorated with blue vases helps to make the orange flowers pop alongside tall silver lanterns to bring a sophisticated candlelight glow. In keeping with the orange color theme, a piece of fruit adorned with a paper green leaf is used as a place card.

This eye-popping colored centerpiece makes a major impact with both the color and array of vase styles.

Above: Using colors such as blue and orange help table décor standout, especially in an outdoor setting where more muted colors can blend in and get lost with the natural elements.

Facing: Uncommon flower displays can add charm and a personal touch at country-style weddings. Items such as this picnic basket are both functional and attractive.

Above, left: Fruit makes for a very functional and budget-friendly place card holder. Oranges, lemons, limes, pears and apples all make great choices.

Above, right: A stark white tablecloth is given a little personality with the addition of blue glasses, illuminated tea lights and copper plates.

Facing: Large multicolored flowers are bundled together to make a bright and cheerful wedding bouquet.

SOURCES

Photography: Sparkle Photography
Venue: Sundance Resort
Event Planner: Soiree Productions
Florist: Artisan Bloom
Makeup: Paula Dahlberg

Fall Harvest

The crisp cool fall season is the main focus of this inspiration shoot and showcases the many details that help to bring the fall season to life. Oranges, browns and golds set the color pallet and work to complement the beautiful and vast Aspen backdrop. No matter what time of year your rustic wedding will take place, the colors and ideas from this fall harvest wedding translate perfectly. From fresh pie to apple cider, this inspiration shoot will leave you looking forward to getting cozy with a warm sweater and enjoying an afternoon outdoors.

Adding seasonal details such as pumpkins, acorns and pears enhance the color palette while looking natural in the surroundings.

a celebration of

Fall

harvest bites and savory sips
thursday, october 20th
5 o'clock
holden marolt barn
aspen, colorado

rsvp to bluebird productions
970.948.7757

Facing, upper left: Adding a small sprig of wheat or pine to your invitations makes them more exciting and brings a seasonal touch.

Facing, upper right: Autumnal flowers stand tall in a vase filled with acorns and is placed next to a tray of apple cider, where real apples serve as the drinking glass.

Facing, lower: A freshly baked pie can be a great alternative to a traditional wedding cake. Small mason jars are perfect for making pie in a jar and then serving it to your guests.

Left: With the Colorado mountains in the distance, this fall inspiration shoot is rich in color and scenery.

Above: An oversized mason jar is the perfect vase for this understated wildflower arrangement.

SOURCES

Photography: Kate Holstein Photography
Venue: Holden Marolt Mining Museum
Event Planner: Bluebird Productions
Florist: The Aspen Branch Studio
Calligrapher: Express Yourself Basalt
Cake: Icing Cakes & Confections

GET THE LOOK

Now that you've explored real weddings and inspiration shoots and decided on a theme or some specific style elements you want to include in your own wedding, you may be wondering how to actually get the look while also incorporating your own style and staying within your budget. Gone are the days when you have to rip out pages from a magazine to start getting ideas for the wedding look you want. We have curated a glorified corkboard with our favorite details for three main types of rustic weddings: vintage rustic, country rustic and woodland rustic. From there, we focus on and break down popular styles such as barn, farm, lakeside, backyard and mountain weddings. By pulling one piece at a time from these detailed storyboards, you will start to see a wonderful wedding take shape. You are, after all, building one layer at a time of your own story, a story that will be told for years to come.

In this section, we walk you through the process to get the look you want for your wedding. By taking the time to carefully select and personalize elements such as the perfect wedding dress, invitations, décor, brides-maid dresses, flowers and more, you will be able to pull together the entire look.

A tree wrapped with family pictures makes for a special photo backdrop.

Vintage Rustic

A vintage-style wedding calls for a mix of a little bit of old and a little bit of new. Finding treasures that have been locked in your mother or grandmother's attic and repurposing them for your wedding day is the perfect place to start. Faded tablecloths, lace doilies, old books, vintage typewriters, mismatched china and tea cups, silver serving pieces, chipped picture frames, and mirrors add elegance and style as well as a little history to the day.

Don't forget to add a bit of flea market fun! Mismatched chairs painted white or in soft faded shades of your color palette add a shabby chic, romantic feel, and inexpensive chandeliers and candelabras add ambiance as well as needed mood lighting.

Vintage bottles, lace doilies and teacups are unconventional centerpieces but look flawless when going for vintage-style décor.

GET THE LOOK: VINTAGE

Flowers: Soft pinks and blush tones bring the vintage theme to life in your flower arrangements. Classic garden flowers such as hydrangeas and peonies are wonderful for both table arrangements and bouquets. Ask your flower designer to show you other examples of heirloom garden flowers that convey the time-worn elegance of a vintage style.

Tabletop: Set your tables with mismatched vintage china, both clear and colored drinking glasses and top it off with lace table runners. Add some dramatic lighting with soft candlelight from crystal candleholders at a variety of heights.

Style Secret: Brought to you by the folks at Anthropologie, BHLDN is no ordinary wedding site. It strives to be different with hcirloom-quality wedding gowns and wedding décor. While it covers some other styles, it seems most rooted in the vintage style.

Great Collectibles: Skeleton keys, typewriters, books, photo frames, old cameras, bikes, watches, suitcases, globes and maps can make a great motif at your vintage wedding.

Right, upper: A small white rustic wedding cake is decorated with a bird's nest cake topper.

Right, lower: Combining different styles of chairs at the same table conveys a flea market type of mood and evokes a vintage chic atmosphere.

MAGGIE'S TIP

No musty attic to explore? Head to Goodwill, church thrift shops, flea markets and your local consignment shops. Not only will your purchases go toward a good cause, but in most cases, you are up-cycling in the most personal way. Hey, no one says it has to be your grandma's lace tablecloth, just someone's grandma's lace tablecloth! Rent vintage china from places such as the Vintage Table Company in Los Angeles, thevintagetableco.com, or Something Borrowed Vintage in Connecticut, someborrowedvintage.com.

Country Rustic:
Farms, Barns, Vineyards & Backyards

An open farm field, a post-and-beam barn, the graceful vines sheltering a vineyard, courtyards, or a pretty backyard—all elements of an elegant country wedding that combine the natural beauty of the setting with the rough-hewn romance of our classic American countryside and backyards. Envision long wood tables filled with soft candlelight in the minimal interior of a barn.

A vineyard dressed up for dining and dancing. A farm field filled with banners and flags heralding the union of a country couple. A backyard can be transformed by Chinese lanterns, soft candlelight and hanging bistro lights.

Below: Hanging lanterns and white lights can make a large venue such as a barn not only feel more intimate, but it can also provide some pleasant mood lighting for the special event.

Facing, left: A long burlap runner with a stitched heart complete with the couple's initials can be a fun DIY project. If sewing is not in your skill set, create a computer-generated lookalike and iron it onto your runners.

Facing, right: Creative seating can be a fun way to make your wedding ceremony all your own. This wedding achieves a classic country feel by using fabric-covered hay bales.

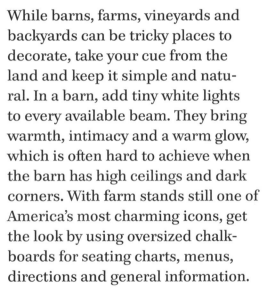

While barns, farms, vineyards and backyards can be tricky places to decorate, take your cue from the land and keep it simple and natural. In a barn, add tiny white lights to every available beam. They bring warmth, intimacy and a warm glow, which is often hard to achieve when the barn has high ceilings and dark corners. With farm stands still one of America's most charming icons, get the look by using oversized chalkboards for seating charts, menus, directions and general information.

Most farm settings celebrate local produce, foods and products. Use as many items as you can from the farm to decorate and incorporate into the meal. Using locally grown food and products is a wonderful way to celebrate and give back to the area. The farm-to-table movement is one that should not be overlooked when planning your country wedding. Add farm baskets, hay bales, chicken wire and

gingham to celebrate the simplicity of the style. While vineyards are already pretty romantic places, you can add to their charm by reaching back to their heritage of oak barrels and French country style complete with wheat bundled as centerpieces and zinc bistro-style place cards. The idea of a backyard wedding is that it is an intimate affair in an intimate space. Use this to your advantage and allow guests to sit where they like for the ceremony and reception. This will convey the idea of what a backyard gathering among friends is supposed to be like.

Just because your wedding is taking place at home does not mean you have to skimp on the elegance. Add a touch of amusement to the festivities by having traditional lawn games available for your guests to play. Guests of all ages will want join in the fun.

Upper, left: Small mason jars tied with ribbon hang from the chairs at an outdoor wedding ceremony.

Upper, right: Be resourceful with displaying your drinks for a backyard party type of feel. Galvanized buckets can be found at hardware stores and are very budget friendly.

Center, left: This menu card is adorned with a small piece of twine and a small fern branch.

Center, right: Old shutters are repurposed into place card displays and are dressed up with large sunflowers at this outdoor wedding.

GET THE LOOK: COUNTRY

Flowers: Use pitchers filled with wildflowers, and don't underestimate the simple beauty of daisies and sunflowers. Oftentimes, the traditional clear vase doesn't seem to fit in these locations, so ask your florist about alternative floral containers such as apple picking baskets.

Tabletop: Simple farm-style tabletop décor can be created as easily as adding burlap table runners, chalkboard place cards and silverware tied with twine. Hang burlap banners from the head table that read: "just married" or "mr. & mrs."

Favors: Send guests home with locally made jam or honey and attach a tag that reads something clever such as "spread the love" or "love is sweet."

Style Secret: Reach out to the local farmers and merchants and use their products in your wedding. Buy pies made from a local bakery and serve them as your desserts.

Facing, lower: A farm table with eight different pies and one small white wedding cake looks like the perfect rustic dessert table.

Upper right: A Mr. & Mrs. burlap banner can be hung above the head table, dance floor or even around the cake table. Banners are easy to make or can be found online at handmade sites like Etsy.com.

Lower right: A piece of burlap stitched with the words "bride" and "groom" are tied to the backs of the wedding couple's chairs.

MAGGIE'S TIP

While these settings can be difficult, they are also often a blank palette. Use this to your advantage. Enlist your creative family members and friends and start adding creative and handmade touches. Not a craft bride? Search online stores such as Etsy for wonderful one-of-a-kind items to enhance these beautiful locations.

Woodland Rustic: Lakeside & Mountain

Being surrounded by nature is usually one reason why couples decide to have a rustic-style wedding. Nothing can add more beauty to a wedding than having a lakeside or mountain wedding. Imagine arriving to your wedding reception by boat and then dining on the shores of the lake. Sounds like a magical and unforgettable experience, right? Let the region inspire your wedding-day décor and name your tables the names of the surrounding lakes or mountains. Add wooden directional signs and camp-style lanterns.

A simple wooden wedding sign stands among the trees in the woods.

GET THE LOOK: WOODLAND

Flowers: If you are having a woodland wedding, think about having large flower arrangements filled with colors inspired by the location. Many times with woodland weddings, the flower arrangements have to be larger in size so they can stand out from the large-scale backdrops. Birch, twigs, berries and pine cones are wonderful additions to flower arrangements.

Tabletop: Add something unique and different to your tables beyond the traditional flower arrangements. Think about adding a camping-style lantern or sprinkling mini acorns down the tables. Tall birch branches can really look amazing when added to a table's flower arrangements as well.

Left: Along with nature-inspired details, this rustic wedding cake sits atop a wooden cake stand. I love the originality of the cake and even the cute details of the heart with the couple's initials in the cake design.

Upper: Long rectangle-shaped tables allow for a more fluid centerpiece décor, one that can continue down the entire table.

Lower: The smallest details can really enhance the overall décor. This mini white pumpkin and handful of acorns really completes the country rustic theme.

Above: Small birch branches help to raise the candles and create a bit of height to the centerpieces.

Left: This Florida outdoor wedding ceremony takes place under a majestic tree.

Favors: Mini fishing creel with candy, hot cocoa mix, compasses and anchors all make for festive woodland rustic wedding favors.

Lakeside: Lakeside lodges and camps offer fun lakeside venues and oftentimes are less expensive than other venues. A canoe paddle painted white makes for a great alternative guestbook, and fill a canoe with ice and let that serve as a beverage center for your guests. Worried about your guests getting cold as the night goes on? Have a cute basket filled with plaid blankets just in case they need to get cozy.

Mountain: Pick a fun motif for your mountain wedding such as crossed skis or a ski patrol–style crest and have it woven into your day by adding it to your save the dates, invitations, ceremony programs and place cards. Ski resorts can often be a perfect venue not just in the winter. Many of them also offer summer wedding spaces. Keep with the ski resort theme and have your place cards look like lift tickets.

Above: A small chalkboard on a miniature easel shows off the table number marked in Roman numerals.

MAGGIE'S TIP

Having an outdoor wedding ceremony is one of the most popular reasons for choosing a woodland rustic setting. While beautiful, these locations provide such a large backdrop that creating an intimate ceremony space is paramount. Adding a focal point in your ceremony site such as a stonewall, a large tree or a birch arbor structure provides the necessary foundation. Arranging your ceremony seating options in a semicircle shape is another great way to bring intimacy to an outdoor ceremony location.

ADVICE & GUIDANCE

We all need a little help when it comes to planning a wedding. Many times we seek advice from people who are emotionally invested in the big day, such as family, friends and bridesmaids. That being said, we often need an additional perspective. One of the most popular features on the blog is the "Ask Maggie" section, where brides get the chance to email me their questions and gather useful advice or resources related to a specific aspect of rustic weddings. This section of the blog is one of my favorites because it allows me to really connect with the community of Rustic Wedding Chic readers. In any given week, I may get requests to help a bride pick out the perfect color palette, decide on a bridesmaid dress, locate the perfect venue and much more. I have put together some of the most frequently asked questions that come from my readers and enlisted the help from a few of my trusted wedding professional friends. Gain insight from Chelsea and Virginia, event planners at Bluebird Productions, and beauty expert Catherine Ianelli from Farm Couture Living.

A Vermont lakeside wedding ceremony displays fall rustic touches, with the birch garden arbor being the main focal point in addition to smaller seasonal details such as a leaf-covered aisle.

What would be the best color palette for the different seasons?

With hundreds of beautiful color combinations to choose from, you may not know where to begin. When creating a color palette for your wedding day, influences to keep in mind include colors you are naturally drawn to, colors that will work for the style of the wedding you are planning and colors of the season your wedding will be in. No matter what season you are planning your wedding for, it is always best to use the natural beauty of the season to complement your wedding style.

SUMMER: Warm temperatures and sunny weather make almost any color look great at a summer wedding, but a few of my favorite colors for the season are navy, light blue, yellow and white. Other great colors include purples, leaf greens, corals, creams, turquoises.

SPRING: With everything in bloom, spring colors really pop when you have a color palette filled with purples, corals and greens and then blend in soft greys and off-whites. Pinks and pewters work well too.

FALL: Dark rich colors such as bronze, orange, green and rust are the perfect colors for a fall wedding.

WINTER: A winter wedding can come to life with color palettes filled with whites, ice blues and golds, or a more festive holiday season wedding can feature dark reds.

A bride with her bridesmaids wearing cowboy boots go for a walk down a country road. Each bridesmaid is wearing a simple black dress with pearls but shows off her own style with her necklace length, hairstyle and boot choice.

How do I pick the best dress for my bridesmaids?

Bridesmaids come in all shapes and sizes and because these women are our closest friends, we want to honor their individuality and celebrate their beauty. The first thing to keep in mind is that you don't have to pick one dress for all the women in your wedding party. Many dress companies now offer several different body styles in the same color. A variety of options will allow you to maintain your wedding's color theme, while also letting your bridesmaids pick the dress silhouette that looks best on them and one that they feel the most comfortable in. Since bridesmaids often pay for their own dresses, giving them a few choices will not only help them find a dress that is comfortable for their figure but will also enable them stay within their budget.

If you are determined to have all your bridesmaids wearing the same style dress, then try to take into account the different body styles in your wedding party and involve everyone in the decision-making process. There is nothing worse than an email from a bride giving you a link to the dress you WILL be wearing in her wedding. If solid colors are not your thing, don't be afraid to consider patterned dresses. They are a little less traditional but might be the perfect complement to your overall wedding décor.

What are the best ways to "dress up" a barn for my barn wedding?

We love barn weddings at Rustic Wedding Chic because of their classic beauty and wonderful versatility. We also understand that no matter how beautiful a barn is on its own, you may want to dress it up a little for your wedding day. The number one thing that adds elegance to a barn location is lighting. Good lighting can set the perfect mood while also adding dramatic touches. The best way to get the most bang for your buck is to hang tiny white lights. By stringing these lights around the barn, you can easily transform it from an everyday space to a gorgeous wedding location. In addition to the strung lights, you can create intimate table settings with small votive candles. Feel free to experiment with the arrangement of the candles by either grouping them together to make a bold statement or spreading them around the table. Mason jars make great candleholders for candles of all sizes. For a beautiful, understated look, fill the mason jars with water and add a floating votive candle. Lighting is just the start to how you can "dress up" a barn for your wedding. Another thing to consider is renting nice chairs and linens for the tables because even small details can automatically upgrade your event from just a get-together to a wedding. Hang long white drapes from the beams to breakup the large space and create a more intimate space.

Below, left: Small white lights enhance the natural barn structure and gives it that something special to make it wedding worthy.

Below, right: This enchanting barn is ready for a wedding with its fall harvest–style entrance décor and low-strung lights for atmosphere.

I just started planning my wedding—what is the best way to start putting my style ideas together?

I often hear from brides or couples who have just started to plan their rustic wedding and they all seem to be wondering the same thing: Where is the best place to start and what's the first step in the planning process? When you first get engaged, it is so exciting and your head is filled with wonderful possibilities and fantasies about what your dream wedding will be. But soon the reality sets in that you need to actually begin planning and that is when I often hear from brides—at that first moment of panic—about where to start. Here are my suggestions for how you can start to plan your rustic wedding.

1. Pick A Season and Three Possible Dates

I know the old idea was to pick a date and then make everything work around that date, but I suggest starting with a season and then picking three dates that work for you, your fiancé and close family and friends involved in the wedding. By having more than just one date in mind, you will have the opportunity to be more flexible when it comes to considerations such as venue availability and work schedules.

2. Put Together a List of Words That Describe Your Dream Wedding

If you are anything like me, you've been imagining your wedding day since the seventh grade, but now you get to make all those dreams become a reality. Before you can get a clear visual idea of your wedding, you need to be able to verbally express what type of wedding you would like. When coming up with words to describe your wedding, try to think about more than just the venue and style. Try to really capture the mood you want for your wedding. For example, if you want to have a relaxed barn wedding, brainstorm all the words related to that one broad term. Another way to generate a list is to think of the words you want your wedding guests to use to describe the day. It's okay if these words change as you go through the planning process. The most important thing is that you have a starting point. Once you have a collection of words and ideas, you can move toward putting together an inspiration board. Close your eyes, picture your dream wedding and write down the words that describe your day. Having a word bank accessible will help you keep your vision alive through the various planning stages.

3. Create an Inspiration Board

After you have decided on the words that will represent your wedding day, it's time to put some visual ideas together. An inspiration board is a wonderful way for you to see how your wedding might come to life. Some brides tell me that they do a separate inspiration board for each aspect of the wedding, including flowers, dresses, colors, cakes and so on. Other brides choose to do one inspiration board that briefly touches on each detail. The website Pinterest is a great resource because it lets you create inspiration boards online by gathering images from any website.

4. Pick a Venue

Many times, the details of a wedding will readily fall into place once you have chosen your wedding venue. For example, when I was planning

my own lakeside wedding, I couldn't decide what type of dinner tables I wanted. I went back and forth between round tables and long, farm-style tables. If only I had known that once I picked the venue where my wedding reception would be held, I had no choice but to go with long tables because that was the only way I was going to fit 225 people into the space. I could have saved myself so many hours of hemming and hawing.

The wedding venue you select will no doubt help you decide what areas of the wedding planning you need to focus on and even help in the decision-making process about some details. For example, if you pick a venue that is not what is considered "full service," meaning that they only offer you the space and you need to rent or provide the rest, then you know that your next task is looking into local rental companies. If your wedding venue is more of a "one stop shopping" kind of venue where everything is provided for you, then you can feel good about moving on to the more fun details such as dress shopping!

Classic country-style chairs accompany long farm-style wedding tables with burlap runners at this barn wedding.

How do I put together a welcome bag for guests?

I have to say, I love a good welcome bag! These bags don't have to be over the top or expensive to be fun. It's all about exercising your inventiveness and giving your guests a wonderful way to start the wedding weekend with you.

There are two key things I think should be in every bag. The first is a welcome note from you and your fiancé, greeting your guests and thanking them for coming to your wedding. The second is an event card. Including an event card will be really helpful for your guests because many times they forget to bring their invitation and don't have the specifics on times and locations. Pictured to the right is an example of welcome bags. For my own wedding, I used kraft gable boxes and added a vintage postcard with a welcome note and a weekend calendar of the events, including times and addresses.

There's no reason why you shouldn't also include a few quirky items for your guests. I suggest starting local.

Find some fun little items from the area to show off the local color. For example, if you were getting married in Door County, Wisconsin, known for its cherries, a little bag of chocolate-covered cherries would be a great way to greet your guests. Water is essential for thirsty travelers, so including a bottle of water would be a much-appreciated addition. Include a local map and visitors guide of the area to encourage your guests to explore and experience all that the wedding location has to offer. Lastly, don't feel that you have to use a bag! Get creative! Other containers such as tote bags, galvanized buckets and picnic baskets can all be used to welcome your guests to your wedding celebration.

TIPS FROM THE PROS

Chelsea VanVleet and Virginia Frischkorn created Bluebird Productions because they saw a need for an environmentally friendly event concierge company in Aspen, Snowmass and the Roaring Fork Valley. After working for many Aspen wedding planners at the various Aspen wedding venues, Chelsea and Virginia noticed the excess waste created as a by-product of the event industry.

Tips for a Western Chic Wedding
By Chelsea VanVleet & Virginia Frischkorn

Choose Your Location: A western-themed affair can be created in almost any setting, but a barn, ranch or fabulous fields are natural choices to make the most of your theme.

Colors: Decide on a color palate for your wedding. With a western theme, you are able to choose from many different colors. Colors can range from bright wildflower colors to muted earth tones.

Think about the Décor: Common western décor has a wide scope. Do you want the horseshoes, cowboy hats and wagon wheels or are you going for the more modern burlap, galvanized buckets and raffia look?

Keep the Décor Clean and Avoid too Much Kitsch: When working with your florist or décor vendor, keep the overall feel clean and avoid things that are too kitschy. This will keep the wedding chic instead of a pure "western" wedding. A little bit of kitsch here and there is fun but find modern twists: ash trays in the shape of donkeys, burlap linens with elegant lace runners, a chandelier created of cowboy hats, etc.

Music: A country band or bluegrass band will add the perfect ambiance to the occasion. If you prefer to have a classic wedding band, why not have a bluegrass band play cocktail hour to get your guests in the spirit?

Guest Attire: Recommend that guests wear cowboy cocktail attire. Guests will not show up in jeans or ball gowns. They will show up in just the right attire for the theme—cowboy boots and dresses, button downs and khakis.

Bridal Attire: A ball gown is typically not the ideal dress for a western wedding. Choose something lighter and more festive. A beautiful lace dress will fit right in. Cowboy boots are the perfect shoes for this theme wedding!

Choose Your Menu: Offer your guests a more refined menu than standard western fair. Dress up the ribs with a unique sauce, serve tenderloin and use a customized brand with your logo to make the meat look fun, or create a fun signature cocktail and serve it in a mason jar.

Paper Goods: Let your guests know they are in for a fabulous and western chic wedding by sending invitations and save the dates with wording such as "we're getting hitched." Invitations can even be printed on burlap or have fun western icons such as ropes, stars and spurs. Be sure to use a creative font!

Tips for a Destination Mountain Wedding

Hire a Planner: If you have the financial resources to hire a full-service planner, planning a wedding from afar can be very stress free. If you do not, we recommend that you hire a day-of planner in order to allow yourself to relax and really enjoy the day. Planners are able to recommend the best local vendors, inform you of the unknown hotspots in the area, handle unforeseen emergencies and allow you to know that your hard work will be executed just the way you desired.

Plan a Trip: Meeting with vendors (especially your officiant and photographer) is very important to make sure your personalities click. You will spend a lot of time on the day of your wedding with your vendors and you want to know that they are great at the job and fabulous people as well!

Save-the-Date: Send out save-the-dates at least six months in advance of your wedding date to give guests ample time to schedule the trip and budget for your wedding.

Deliver Gift Bags: Gift bags do not have to be expensive, but having a gift bag waiting for guests when they arrive is a nice start to an exciting event. Write a personal note letting guests know that you appreciate their efforts in traveling to your wedding. Also, be sure to include an itinerary for the week or weekend, a local map (normally free at the Chamber of Commerce), local restaurant guides and a gift from the area such as local honey, tea, granola, etc.

Drink Water: Altitude affects many people differently, especially older guests. Drinking lots of water can help deter altitude sickness. Remind guests that this may be a problem and that they should be over hydrated before and during their stay. Additionally, ask your caterer to pass around water on a tray prior to the ceremony along with any other beverages you may be offering.

Most of your guests have probably traveled from far and wide to come to the wedding and want to experience all that this mountain destination has to offer as well as attend your nuptials. Schedule some fun events that are special to the area such as a hike, a bike ride or whitewater rafting.

Bridal Attire: Remember that you will normally have to travel on a chairlift or in a gondola with your dress. On most occasions, there is a place to change close to the ceremony site, so wear comfortable clothes and choose a dress that is manageable and does

not take up the entire gondola or chairlift for your getaway!

Guest Attire: Remind your guests to wear flat shoes because they may be walking a distance on gravel paths or through grass, which stilettoes would likely sink through. Also inform your guests that mountain weather can change in the blink of an eye! Additionally, mountain locations often have lovely ceremony sites on top of mountains where the temperatures are 20 degrees less than towns. Guests may want to bring a coat, hat and gloves (depending on the season).

Wear Sunscreen: The sun can be very intense on top of a mountain, and out West, you are closer to the sun and burn much more easily. Have sunscreen on hand and remind guests to wear plenty during an outdoor ceremony.

Don't Forget to Eat: No one wants a bride passing out on the top of a mountain. Eat a healthy breakfast, even if you don't usually eat breakfast, as you may not eat again until the reception. Ask your caterer and planner to have snacks on hand just in case!

TIPS FROM A BEAUTY EXPERT

Catherine Ianelli is a celebrity esthetician, visionary alchemist and founder of Farm Couture Living, a boutique skincare and fragrance company. She is known for her vibrant esthetic style and signature Farm Couture Facial. Catherine meticulously collaborates with local farms, horticulturalists and artisans to provide her clientele with the highest quality of hand-tailored gourmet skincare.

Timeless Beauty

By Catherine Ianelli

On your wedding day, you will of course be the center of attention and focus for your groom, family and friends. This incredibly special day is your day to shine. Flawless vibrant skin is completely possible for you and your bridal party, if you begin a simple skincare regime a few months prior to your wedding day. We all know that getting married can be a stressful time, but it's crucial that you start to take care of your skin, so you can feel more confident and beautiful on your journey to wedding bliss.

As a bride, you will be working intimately with your photographer and your pictures will be greatly enhanced if your skin is as stunning as your dress. If you focus on pampering your skin, you will also be building a beautiful canvas for your makeup application that day. When it comes to wedding-day makeup, less is usually more, and you want to naturally highlight your glowing skin. Having clear skin allows for more of "you" to be timelessly captured.

Below you will find a hand-selected boutique collection of expert tips, featuring the crème of the harvest to ensure you will be nothing less than farm couture beautiful.

Farm Couture Facial: I recommend getting monthly facials six months prior to the wedding date, but if you can't make it to your favorite esthetician, then I have a DIY list of easy recipes to get you farm couture fabulous!

Farm Fresh Clean: You want to have dewy, radiant lustrous skin on the day of your wedding and of course for your awaited honeymoon, so brides need to start with a great facial cleanser. You want to make sure that you are removing your makeup each evening and removing all traces of impurities with a gentle cleanser. I recommend doing a daily morning and nighttime double-cleanse routine, meaning wash your face twice to ensure you are thoroughly removing all impurities.

FARM COUTURE TIP

After washing your face, splash a little cold water on your face to close pores. This also adds an instant natural glow! I recommend using a milk-based cleanser, as milk is a natural skin softener and a gentle exfoliant.

Oh Honey, Bee Mine: Honey is simply amazing! It's a hundred percent natural, anti-aging and leaves skin soft, hydrated and instantly nourished. Honey is also antibacterial, so it's fabulous for brides with problematic, sensitive skin. Before you apply the mask, splash your face with warm water to open pores. Spread the mask evenly on your face, avoiding the eyes, and leave it on for fifteen to thirty minutes. Rinse off with a soft material such as cheesecloth or a soft towel. Using this once a week will leave your skin glowing and oh so sweet!

FARM COUTURE TIP

I recommend using raw honey, as it is pure and has not been pasteurized or filtered, and is taken directly from the hive.

RESORCES

All websites listed in this book are accurate at the time of publication but are subject to change.

BEAUTY

Erin McKenna: Paragon Studios, Shelburne, VT, 802.985.9119

Farm Couture Living: farmcoutureliving.com

Hair Daze: hdaze.com

Makeup Artists Guild: makeupartistguild.com

Pamela Lesch Makeup: makeupartistcharleston.com

Paula Dahlberg: paulajdahlberg.com

Stella Nova: stella-nova.com

CATERING & CAKE SERVICES

Bad Bones BBQ: grabyourpork.com

Fresh Flavors: freshflavorscatering.com

Good Food Catering: goodfoodcatering.net

Harvest Moon Catering: hmcatering.com

Icing Cakes and Confections: icingaspen.com

Lake Sunapee Country Club: lakesunapeecc.com

Patty Cakes: pattycakes-tn.com

The Cupcake Lounge: thecupcakeloungeok.com

EVENT PLANNERS & DESIGNERS

Blue Lemon Provisions: bluelemonprovisions.com

Bluebird Productions: bluebirdaspen.com

Claire Bean Floral & Event Design: clairebean.com

Events by Shelbi Rene: eventsbyshelbirene.com

Peacock Events: peacockeventscharleston.com

Soiree Productions: soireeproductions.com

FLORAL DESIGNS

Art of Nature: natureswildart.com

Artisan Bloom: artisanbloom.com

Blomma Flicka: blommaflicka.com

Branch Design Studio: branchdesignstudio.com

Claire Bean Floral & Event Design: clairebean.com

Clines Florist: clinesfloristnc.com

Crystal Marie's Floral: Minocqua, WI, 715.356.6644

Sugar Magnolias: naturecomposed.com

The Aspen Branch: aspenbranch.com

The Bloom Room: bloom-room.com

INVITATIONS, STATIONERY & CALLIGRAPHY

Dancing Pen & Press: etsy.com/shop/DancingPenandPress

Designs in Paper: designsinpaper.com

Express Yourself Basalt: expressyourselfbasalt.com

Griffin-vites: griffin-vites.com

Shindig Invitations: shindiginvites.com

The Paper Source: paper-source.com

The Village Invites: villageinvites.com

Three By The Quill Pen: three45.squarespace.com

Wedding Chicks: weddingchicks.com

PHOTOGRAPHERS & PHOTO CREDITS

Ash and James Photography: blog.ashandjames
photography.com
Work shown on pages 16–27

Brklyn View Photography: brklynview.com
Work shown on pages 3, 7 (left and right), 138, 150,
and back cover (lower left)

Carrie Wildes: carriewildes.com
Work shown on pages 13 (left), 134, 140 (top left), 144 (bottom)

Charlie Panian: 3guysred.com
Work shown on page 153

ee Photography: eephotome.com
Work shown on pages 1, 6, 8, 10 (upper), 14, 84–91, 102, 112–23,
136, 137 (lower), 139, 140 (top right), 141 (top and bottom), 149,
152, front cover, and back cover (top right)

Hinkley Photo: hinkleyphoto.com
Work shown on pages 7 (center), 13 (right), 140 (middle right),
and back cover (top left)

Holm, Tahni Candelaria: joyeusephotography.com
Work shown on pages 72–83, 142

Jason + Heather Barr, Revival Photography:
revivalphotography.com
Work shown on pages 64–71

Kate Holstein Photography: kateholstein.com
Work shown on pages 130–33, 154

Krista Lee Photography: kristaleephotography.com
Work shown on pages 28–35, and back cover (lower right)

Kristyn Hogan: kristynhogan.com
Work shown on pages 104–11

Maggie Carson Romano: mcr-photography.com

Mirelle Carmichael Photography: mirellecarmichael.com
Work shown on page 143 (left)

Orchard Cove Photography: orchardcovephotography.com
Work shown on pages 36–45, 92–101, 143 (top right and bottom
right), 146, and author's photo

Our Labor of Love Photography: ourlaboroflove.com
Work shown on pages 10 (lower), 46–63, 137 (top), 140 (bottom
right), 144 (top), 145, and back cover (middle left)

Sparkle Photography: sparklephoto.com
Work shown on pages 124–29

Tom Moore Photo: tommoorephoto.com
Work shown on pages 157, 158

Vanessa Joy Photography: vanessajoy.com
Work shown on pages 9, 140 (middle left)

RENTAL COMPANIES

Classic Party Rentals: classicpartyrentals.com

Lakes Region Tent & Event: lakesregiontent.com

Something Borrowed Vintage: someborrowedvintage.com

The Vintage Table Co.: thevintagetableco.com

Vermont Tent Company: vermonttent.com

VENUES

Basin Harbor Club: basinharbor.com

Biltmore: biltmore.com

Bishop Farm Bed & Breakfast: bishopfarm.com

Cedarwood: historiccedarwood.com

Crossed Keys Inn: crossedkeys.com

Doc & Merle Watson Theatre

Holden Marolt Mining Museum: aspenhistorysociety.com/
groundrentals.html

Inn at Westwood Farm: innatwestwoodfarm.com

Sundance Resort: sundanceresort.com

The Thomas Bennett House:
governorthomasbennetthouse.com

Wolffer Estate Vineyard: wolffer.com

YMCA Camp Nawakwa: ymcachicago.org/nawakwa

OTHER

aPearantly Sew: apearantlysew.bigcartel.com

BHLDN: bhldn.com

Etsy: etsy.com

J.Crew: jcrew.com

Pinterest: pinterest.com

Vermont Photobooth Company: vermontphotobooth.com

Vermont Rustic Cedar: vermontrusticcedar.com

Watters: watters.com

Whispering Pines Catalog: whisperingpinescatalog.com